ALFRED's
SACRED PERFORMER
COLLECTIONS

MW00784706

A Romantic-Style Christmas

10 Expressive Arrangements Inspired by Chopin

Arranged by Faye López

What is more beautiful than a flawless rendition of a Chopin prelude or nocturne, performed with heartfelt emotion? Because I have played, taught, and loved Chopin's piano music over the years, I was thrilled to arrange a Christmas piano collection inspired by Chopin's well-loved works. It is a joy to study his scores and borrow ideas from his artistic "palette," weaving his ideas in with my own. The collection includes arrangements with quotations from Chopin's "Nocturne in E Minor" and "Prelude in D-flat Major" ("Raindrop"), as well as other beloved Chopin pieces.

Enjoy the rich heritage of classics and Christmas carols as you explore the arrangements in *A Romantic-Style Christmas*!

Faye López

Alfred Music
P.O. Box 10003
Van Nuys, CA 91410-0003
alfred.com

ISBN-10: 1-4706-1732-3
ISBN-13: 978-1-4706-1732-5

Cover Photo
Christmas tree decoration: © Shutterstock.com / fotorutkowscy

Coventry Carol
(Inspired by Chopin's Nocturne in E Minor, Op. 72, No. 1)

Traditional
Arr. Faye López

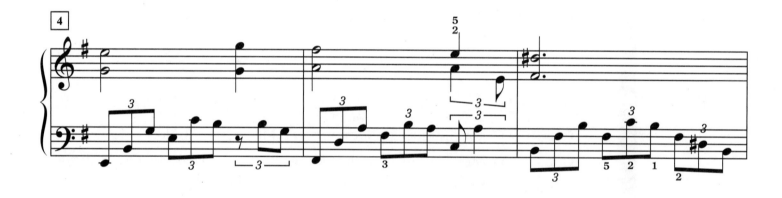

3

4

God Rest Ye Merry, Gentlemen

(Inspired by Chopin's Prelude in E Minor, Op. 28, No. 4)

Traditional
Arr. Faye López

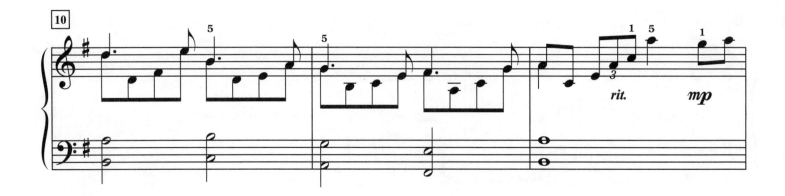

In the Bleak Midwinter

(Inspired by Chopin's Prelude in G Major, Op. 28, No. 3)

Gustav Holst
Arr. Faye López

12

Joy to the World

(Inspired by Chopin's Polonaise in A-flat Major, Op. 53, "Heroic")

G. F. Handel

Arr. Faye López

O Come, All Ye Faithful

(Inspired by Chopin's Ballade in G Minor, Op. 23, No. 1)

John F. Wade
Arr. Faye López

Once in Royal David's City
(Inspired by Chopin's Etude in E Major, Op. 10, No. 3)

Henry J. Gauntlett
Arr. Faye López

Rise Up, Shepherd, and Follow
(Inspired by Chopin's Prelude in F Major, Op. 28, No. 23)

Spiritual
Arr. Faye López

Still, Still, Still

(Inspired by Chopin's Prelude in D-flat Major, Op. 28, No. 15, "Raindrop")

Traditional
Arr. Faye López

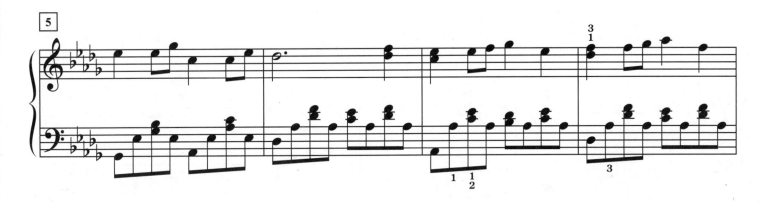

(Approx. Performance Time – 2:15)

There's a Song in the Air
(Inspired by Chopin's Nocturne in E-flat Major, Op. 9, No. 2)

Karl P. Harrington
Arr. Faye López

What Child Is This?
(Inspired by Chopin's Nocturne in C-sharp Minor, posthumous)

Traditional
Arr. Faye López